MAP
to
MATURITY

MAP
to
MATURITY

A BELIEVER'S GUIDE TO GROWING
TOWARDS CHRISTIAN MATURITY

Mark H. Ballard

NORTHEASTERN BAPTIST PRESS

Bennington, Vermont

Map to Maturity
A Believer's Guide to Growing Towards Christian Maturity
Copyright © 2024 by Mark H. Ballard

Published by Northeastern Baptist Press
        Post Office Box 4600
        Bennington, VT 05201

Softcover ISBN: 978-1-953331-35-9

To Cindy and Ben

TABLE OF CONTENTS

CHAPTER 1

Making Sure
You're on the Right Road

When I was a young boy, my family went on a trip from Colorado to Oregon. To this young boy it was the greatest adventure one could possibly take part in. Dad had installed a new Citizen Band Radio (CB) in the car, and I imagined myself talking with truckers all the way to Oregon and back. It was going to be one of the most exciting things I had ever done.

Early in the trip I remember wondering how my dad could possibly know how to get to a place so far away. I knew he had a map, but he did not seem to look at it very often. After what seemed to me like days of driving, we arrived at our destination.

Dad, my uncles, and my older brother had discussed the possibility of returning home in another direction. I had mixed feelings about that, but thought it would be nice to see some things we had missed on the trip up. Besides, I really had no choice in the matter, I was just along for the ride. I asked Dad if we could possibly go through the edge of California so we could say we had been there. We were on somewhat of a time schedule, so Dad decided against the idea.

We had been traveling down the highway headed for Utah for quite some time. Having been through several towns and much open country, my brother began to get concerned. He spoke up, indicating we might have missed our turn. The possibility was discussed and then dismissed, and we continued down the road. After a while my dad became concerned. Finally, we stopped and pulled out that big old map. It was soon discovered that we had missed our road and had gone nearly 40 miles out of our way. We almost saw California after all, as we were not far from the border. We had to turn around because we discovered that we were on the wrong road, and if we continued going in the same direction we would never get to Utah.

ROADS PEOPLE TRAVEL

Many people experience a similar situation in their spiritual journey. They want to move towards Christian maturity, yet they are on the wrong road. Some who think themselves to be Children of God are actually traveling down the wrong highway. The fact is, though many people consider themselves to be Christians, there is wide disagreement concerning the definition of Christianity. Many people claiming to be Christians are on different roads, yet they are all trying to reach Christian maturity and ultimately an eternal home in Heaven.

One might assume that the author is referring to the various denominations of the Christian faith. However, many times people within the same denomination disagree as to the proper road to travel. Though there may be several roads that could be named, there really are only three possible roads to travel. We will call the first road *Unbelief Boulevard*. The second road some folks travel is *Self-Righteous Street*. *Belief Way* is the third road.

Unbelief Boulevard

Unbelief Boulevard is a road with three lanes. Though at first glance the following groups may seem to be on a different road altogether, they are in reality, on the same road of unbelief. Traveling the first lane are those who have chosen a religious system other than Biblical Christianity. These folks might be Jewish, Muslim, Hindu, or one of the other many religions of the world. Though they have a religious belief system, it is not compatible with what God has revealed in His Word, the Bible.

The second lane is full of folks referred to as agnostics. These have adopted a philosophy that says they are unsure whether God exists. Some are *seeking agnostics*, some are *convinced agnostics*, and others have a religious affiliation but are *practicing agnostics*. A seeking *agnostic* claims to be open to the idea of the existence of God, but they are seeking further proof before they will commit their lives to Him. The *convinced agnostic* is someone who has determined that there really is no way to know if God exists until death. These people have determined to live their lives as skeptics. The *practicing agnostic* is one who has a claimed religious affiliation, but lives as though God really does not exist.

The third lane of *Unbelief Boulevard* is for travelers who consider themselves to be atheist. By definition, an atheist is one who does not believe in the existence of God. Though the atheist movement in America made a lot of noise in the 1960's and 70's, the actual number of atheists in this country remains very small. It is reported that 81% of Americans claim to believe in God.[1] This author has never met a real atheist. There are people who claim atheism as their philosophy, but after very little discussion they admit that they are really in the agnostic lane.

No matter which lane one is traveling, all those on *Unbelief Boulevard* will end up at the same destination. The Bible refers to this destination as *destruction*. If you are traveling down *Unbelief Boulevard* exit immediately and turn to Christ in faith while you still have opportunity.

Self-Righteous Street

Another road some people travel in an attempt to reach Christian maturity and the Heavenly Home is *Self-Righteous Street*. This is without a doubt, the broadest street in the world. Most people find themselves traveling down this road at one time or another. Those on *Self-Righteous Street* believe that they must work their way to Heaven.

Though this road may have many lanes, all have the same basic construction. Each lane has a list of certain good works to perform and bad actions to avoid. Some lanes put more emphasis on the good works accomplished, while others put the emphasis on bad deeds avoided. No matter which of these lanes an individual is in, it is believed if one does more good than bad, they will be admitted into Heaven.

Jesus said, "Enter by the narrow gate; for wide is the gate and broad is the way that leads to destruction, and there are many who go in by it. Because narrow is the gate and difficult is the way which leads to life, and there are few who find it" (Matt 7:13-14, NKJV). In order to understand what the "broad way" is, one must look to the entirety of the New Testament. When this study is made one finds repeatedly, an individual does not enter Heaven by accomplishment of good works or by avoidance of bad actions. Titus 3:5 states, "Not by works of righteousness which we have done, but according to His mercy He saved us, through the washing of regeneration and renewing of the Holy Spirit."

Just as my family thought we were on our way to Utah, but were really headed to California; one can sincerely believe himself to be on the right road to Heaven, yet at the end of life find out that they traveled the wrong path. If you find yourself on *Self-Righteous Street* exit now.

Belief Way

The third road some people travel towards Christian maturity and the Eternal Home is the road of faith. Numerous Scripture references confirm that this is the road the Bible says one must travel. Jesus said, "The time is fulfilled, and the Kingdom of God is at hand. Repent, and *believe* in the Gospel" (Mark 1:15, emphasis added). On another occasion Jesus said, "Most assuredly, I say to you, he who **believes** in Me has everlasting life (John 6:4)." The Apostle Paul echoed Jesus' statements when he told the Philippian jailer, "**Believe** on the Lord Jesus Christ, and you will be saved, you and your household" (Acts 16:31). Further discussion of this road is found below.

5

THE WAY

Just prior to His arrest, trial, death, and resurrection Jesus was speaking to His followers of His going away. He told them that He was going to prepare a Heavenly Home for them. Thomas, one of the twelve disciples, said they did not know the way to get to this great home Jesus was describing. "Jesus said to him, 'I am the way, the truth, and the life. No one comes to the Father except through me'" (John 14:6).

In the above sentence Jesus used the Greek word *odos* translated here as *way*. *Odos* can be defined as a road, path, or way. Notice also *way* is preceded by the definite article. In response to Thomas' question, Jesus stated that He is the only true road to the Father and the Eternal Home. He then re-emphasized His statement by adding, "no one comes to the Father except through me." It can be observed from Jesus Himself, that all other roads are inadequate and will fail to get us to our desired destination.

The fact is, God loves us and created us to have fellowship with Him, but the entrance of sin in our lives has broken that fellowship. The Bible says, "All have sinned and come short of the glory of God" (Rom 3:23). There are all kinds of ways we sin. The Bible speaks of sins of commission, sins of omission, and sin of thoughts. Sins of commission refer to doing things that we should not do. These would include lying, cheating, stealing, etc. Sins of omission refer to not doing what we should. Omission sins would include not loving our neighbor, not reading the Bible, not attending church, etc. Sins of thought are what Jesus referred to when he said, "You have heard that it was said to those of old, 'You shall not commit adultery.' But I say to you that whoever looks at a woman to lust for her has committed adultery with her in his heart" (Matt 5:27-28).[2]

The Scriptures also teach us that sin must be judged. "For the wages of sin is death..." (Rom 6:23a) God is Holy and Just, therefore, He must punish sin. That punishment is spiritual death. Spiritual death will ultimately end in eternal separation from God in Hell. According to the Bible, all of us deserve to be judged because of our disobedience towards God.

The good news is, God loves us so much that He made a way for us to be forgiven of sin and to have a right relationship with Him. This is where Jesus enters the picture. He loved us so much that He left the glory of Heaven, and came to earth to be born in a humble manger. He lived a perfect life, refusing to yield to temptation. Finally, He went to the cross, died in our place, taking the penalty for the things we do wrong. He then rose again defeating sin, death, and the grave. Today He sits at the right hand of the Father, and offers forgiveness of sin to all who believe on Him.

When the Bible says we must believe on Jesus, it means we must trust Him, totally rely on Him, to forgive us and to give us a home in Heaven. It is more than just believing facts about Jesus; we must truly trust Him alone for forgiveness. We must transfer our trust from self to Christ alone. We must admit to Him we cannot be perfect, that we sin and fall short of His plan for our life. Then we must turn to Him in faith, trusting Jesus alone for eternal life. This act of faith is the on-ramp to *Belief Way*.

WHICH ROAD ARE YOU ON?

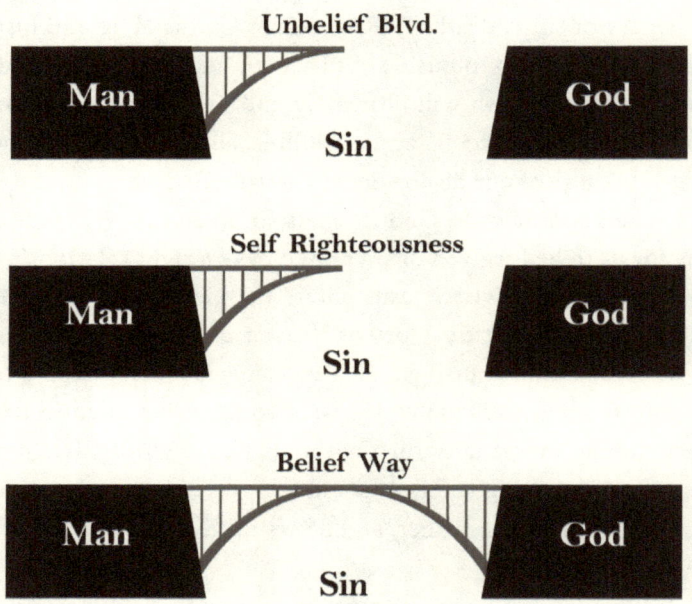

Stop! Spend a few moments evaluating which road you are on. As illustrated in the drawings above, only one road bridges the gap between Man and God.[3] If you are not on "Belief Way" you need to change roads. You can do so right now. Simply turn to Jesus in prayer confessing your sin and transfer your trust from self to Christ. Below is a sample prayer:

> Dear Jesus, I know that I have sinned and deserve to be judged for my actions. I know there is no way I can

be good enough to gain eternal life. I believe that You are the perfect God-Man, that you died in my place, and rose from the dead; so that I could be forgiven of my sin, enter into a right relationship with you, and receive the assurance of eternal life. Right now, I ask you to forgive me of my sin and come into my life. I no longer trust my good works, but I trust You. In Your Name I pray, Amen.

If you made this decision from your heart good news awaits you. "Most assuredly, I say to you, he who believes in Me has everlasting life" (John 6:47). Jesus has given you eternal life. Life that is eternal can never be taken away. Congratulations! You are now on the road to Christian maturity and are traveling down *Belief Way*.

TRAVELING THE ROAD TO MATURITY

Now that you are on the right road you must make sure you do not spend your time stalled out on the shoulder. You want to progress toward your destination of Christian maturity. Many Christians spend years sitting on the shoulder of the road because they are unaware of either the importance of growth, or how to grow.

The Apostle Peter concluded his second epistle with a call for growth. "But grow in the grace and knowledge of our Lord and Savior Jesus Christ. To Him be the glory both now and forever. Amen" (2 Peter 3:18). The author of Hebrews echoed the call to growth. "Therefore, leaving the discussion of the elementary principles of Christ, let us go on to perfection, not laying again the foundation of repentance from dead works and of faith toward God" (Heb 6:1). The Lord expects us to grow towards maturity. The remainder of this book is dedicated to providing a map one can follow as they travel down *Belief Way*. There are several essential stops that must be made on a regular basis if we are to mature properly.

DISCUSSION QUESTIONS

1. What are the three roads that people can travel?
2. Describe *Unbelief Boulevard*.
3. Describe *Self-Righteous Street*.
4. Which road do you think most people are traveling?
5. How can one get on *Belief Way*?
6. What is the final destination of those traveling *Belief Way*?

CHAPTER 2

The Bible is Basic

While traveling down *Belief Way* there are several stops one must make if he/she is to move towards Christian maturity. If you were to set out on a trip from Portland, Maine to San Diego, California there are several stops you would need to make along the road. You would take regular breaks for gas, food, rest, etc. In the same way, if one wants to grow into a mature Christian he/she must make regular stops while traveling *Belief Way*. Time with the Bible is one of the most important stops along life's journey.

The Apostle Paul was in prison awaiting execution for preaching the Gospel when he wrote his young associate for the second time. He knew his life was nearing an end and was not sure he would see Timothy again. Paul tells Timothy that as the last days before Jesus' return to earth grow closer, the times will get worse. People will get more self-centered and less God-centered. Many people will be led astray, even religious people. In the midst of an atmosphere that hinders Christian growth, Timothy was to remain faithful and continue on the path to maturity. This growth would be made possible through "the Holy Scriptures" (2 Tim 3:15).

Why were the Scriptures the key to Timothy's continued growth? How were they going to impact his growth process? What would be the result of Timothy spending time with the Scriptures? The Apostle answered these questions in the last two verses of the chapter.

> All Scripture is given by inspiration of God, and is profitable for doctrine, for reproof, for correction, for instruction in righteousness, that the man of God may be complete, thoroughly equipped for every good work (2 Tim 3:16-17).

This passage indicates three reasons the Bible should be a regular stop for those traveling *Belief Way*. The first reason is because of the *Origin of Scripture*. The second reason has to do with the *Action of Scripture*. The final reason for making time with the Bible a regular priority is because of the *Outcome of Scripture*. Once these issues have been examined, the remaining pages of this chapter will concentrate on the *Exposure to Scripture*.

THE ORIGIN OF SCRIPTURE

The single most important factor in choosing a good book has to do with authorship. The origin of a book will determine its value. The author must have knowledge of his subject and the ability to communicate that knowledge to the reader. The Author is what makes the Bible the most unique book of all time. God Himself is the Author of Holy Scripture. Though He used human hands to communicate His Truth, it is clear that the Bible finds Its origin in God.

Notice the words of the text. **"All Scripture is given by inspiration of God...."** This short phrase communicates eternal truths with eternal implications. First, it speaks to the *extent* of Biblical inspiration. Then it speaks to the *explanation* of Biblical inspiration.

A preacher once stated that he knew a man who believed the Bible was "inspired in spots and he was inspired to spot the spots." Many people have adopted this attitude today. Some would argue that the Bible is inspired only in areas of religious truth. These people would claim that historical or scientific references may or may not be accurate, yet overall, the Bible is inspired to communicate spiritual truth.

Notice the first word of verse 16, "All". This means every passage of the Bible is inspired by God. From the story of creation in Genesis 1 to the description of the eternal state in Revelation 22, the Bible finds Its origin in God. Therefore, when we speak of the *extent of inspiration* it must be admitted that the Bible itself claims to be fully inspired by the Lord. Having established the extent of inspiration let us move on to an *explanation* of the meaning of Biblical inspiration.

There are six views of inspiration that people have held over the years. These are the Natural View, the Illumination View, the Dynamic View, the Neo-Orthodox View, the Mechanical Dictation View, and the Verbal-Plenary View. Each of these are defined below:

» The Natural View - There is no supernatural element to Scripture. The Bible is simply an "inspiring" book of literature.

» The Illumination View – The Bible is Spirit – inspired writings on the same level as any of history's, or today's, spirit-inspired books.

» The Dynamic (Partial) View – The Bible contains the Word of God and is without error and true in areas of doctrine and salvation. It may contain errors in areas of science, history, etc.

» The Neo - Orthodox View – The Bible is inspired but not without error due to the human element. The Bible becomes the Word of God to us in personal experience.

» The Mechanical Dictation View – The writers were passive instruments of God like a typewriter to a typist.

» The Verbal / Plenary View – God superintended the human authors so that in their own words through their individual personalities the Scriptures are inspired fully, to the very words, and are without error in all that they affirm.[4]

In order to determine which of these views are correct according to the testimony of Scripture Itself, let us consider the text at hand. Some additional key and supportive texts will be listed as well.

The word "inspiration" in 2 Timothy 3:16 is a translation of the Greek word *Theopneustos*. Literally the word means *God-breathed*. The idea is that God breathed out the words of Scripture. The words of the Bible are God's Words. The Apostle Peter summed it up in his second epistle, "for prophecy never came by the will of man, but holy men of God spoke as they were moved by the Holy Spirit" (2 Peter 1:21). God breathed the words He wanted to communicate to the heart and mind of the human author who wrote the words on the page using his own writing style and yet communicating the exact words that the Lord intended. Therefore, inspiration is the supernatural operation of the Holy Spirit who, through the different personalities and literary styles of the chosen human authors, invested the very words of the original 66 books of Holy Scripture, alone and in their entirety, as the very Word of God without error in all that they teach (including history and science) and is thereby the infallible rule and final authority for the faith and practice of all believers.

The only view of inspiration that is consistent with the claim of the Bible Itself is the Verbal / Plenary View. The Scriptures claim that inspiration extends to every word of the 66 Books. In other words, the Bible is fully inspired. The word translated "inspiration" in 2 Timothy 3:16 means "God-Breathed" and indicates verbal inspiration. Some additional passages of Scripture which confirm this view are Matthew 5:17-18, John 10:35, Deuteronomy 18:18, 2 Samuel 23:2, 2 Chronicles 34:14, Zechariah 7:12, Matthew 22:43, Acts 4:24-25, and Hebrews 4:7.

The Bible has Its origin in God Himself. It is completely true and reliable. Because the Bible comes from God it is not only trustworthy, but it is profitable for the action it performs and the outcome it produces in our lives.

The Action of Scripture

The text at hand indicates four things the Bible accomplishes in the lives of Its readers. It is "profitable for doctrine, for reproof, for correction, for instruction in righteousness,". "Doctrine" is defined as teaching. Specifically in this text it refers to Christian teaching. All doctrine is to flow from Scripture. What we believe and what we teach must come from the Bible Itself. Human opinion may be right or may be wrong, but God's Word is always true. Where doctrinal traditions conflict with the Word of God they must be changed to reflect the Word of God.

"Reproof" has to do with showing us where we have gone wrong. As we are traveling down *Belief Way* we occasionally make wrong choices and get off track. As we spend time in the Word we are confronted with our shortcomings. Reproof says, "Stop! You are headed the wrong way."

"Correction" refers to the fact that the Bible not only tells us where we go wrong, but also how to get right. If *reproof* says we are headed in the wrong direction, *correction* communicates how we can turn around and go in the right direction.

"Instruction in Righteousness" is the action the Scripture performs when it tells us how to live right in the future. The Bible teaches us how to live a righteous life before God by instructing us in what is right and what is wrong. God's Word serves as a tutor helping us to understand what actions glorify the Lord and what actions fall short of His glory. This instruction comes in the form of both direct commandments and distinct principles that guide us daily as we travel down *Belief Way*.

It is important that we spend time with God's Word regularly because of its origin and because of its action. The Bible is truly the Word of God and is without error. The Scriptures perform four actions that are essential to the growth of a believer. The Bible tells us what to believe and teach; It tells us when we are wrong; It tells us how to get right; and It tells us how to stay right.

The Outcome of Scripture

Every human action brings about a corresponding consequence. The same is true with the action of Scripture. The outcome of God's Word working in the life of the believer is two-fold. First, we see from the text that the Bible makes us complete. Then we see that It equips us for "every good work." In other words, the Scriptures work in our lives to bring us to Christian maturity. Thus, time in the Word is an essential stop on *Belief Way*.

God is at work through His Word to bring us to maturity. A believer who spends time in the Bible will grow as a Christian. Just as a child must be fed a nutritious diet to grow physically, so the believer must be fed a nutritious diet of spiritual food from the Scriptures if he/she is to grow towards maturity. God uses time in the Word to teach, reprove, correct, and instruct us, thus causing growth.

Part of the process of bringing the believer to maturity is to equip him. It is one thing to issue a command and quite another to equip an individual to fulfill that command. Imagine being hired to build a house without having the tools to do the job. You can know what you are to do and even have an idea of how to do it. However, if you do not have the equipment to do the work, the job will not get done. The Bible not only tells us what to do; It also equips us for the job by giving us the tools necessary to live the Christian life.

Time spent with the Bible is an essential stop for the person traveling "Belief Way" because of Its *Origin,* Its *Action,* and Its *Outcome.* If this stop is truly essential, then one must make *Exposure* to the Word a high priority in one's daily life. The final section of this chapter lists ways you can expose yourself to the Bible on a regular basis.

THE EXPOSURE TO SCRIPTURE

1. Through personal Bible reading on a daily basis.
    A. *The Psalm Plan* – Read one Psalm every day, reflect on the meaning, and ask God to help you apply it to your life.
    B. *The Proverb Plan* - Read one Proverb every day (there are 31 Chapters in Proverbs – one for every day of the month), reflect on the meaning, and ask God to help you apply it to your life.
    C. *The Chapter Plan* – Pick a book of the Bible like the Gospel of John and read one chapter each day until you are finished with the book and then move on to another book of the Bible.
    D. *The Year Plan* – There are several Bible reading plans where you can read the Bible through in one year. You can find one on the *You Version Bible* phone app.
2. Through personal Bible memory.
3. Through personal Bible study.

4. Through personal devotional reading.
5. Through sermons at church.
6. Through small group Bible study.
7. Through Christian radio and television.

Discussion Questions

1. What are the three main reasons for the Bible being an essential stop as one travels *Belief Way*?
2. What does the Bible teach about Its origin?
3. What is Biblical Inspiration?
4. What are the four main actions of Scripture?
5. What is the two-fold outcome of the work of the Word in one's life?
6. What are some of the ways that I am presently being exposed to the Bible?
7. How am I going to expose myself more to the Word in the days ahead?

CHAPTER 3

Prayer Must be a Priority

Imagine you are planning a trip from Maine to Florida for the month of January. You have planned to travel I-95 and have determined each stop you will make on the trip. Then you receive a phone call from the White House Chief of Staff. He explains that several people from all over the United States have been randomly selected to attend a town-hall style meeting with the President in the Green Room of the White House. The meeting is to take place January 5th from 4-6 PM.

Though this stop was not in your schedule, you decide to accept the invitation. Why? This is the President of the United States. You realize this is a privilege few Americans ever receive. You know this is an important meeting and you may have an opportunity to express your opinion about a few issues dear to your heart. You realize you have received this invitation from one of the most powerful men in the world. All things considered, you decide to adjust your plans and to make this stop a priority.

Upon acceptance of the invitation, you are informed of several procedural issues that must be dealt with. Over the next several weeks you receive letters, phone calls, and even a visit by a White House employee to prepare you for the visit. On January 5 you are to arrive two hours early in order to take part in a briefing that will prepare you for the proper procedures of spending the evening with the President.

If you are traveling *Belief Way*, you have a standing invitation to be in the presence of the most Important Person of all time and eternity. The Lord God of Heaven is waiting for you to make prayer a priority. He is the One who truly holds all power; therefore, it is a privilege, and it is important to spend time with Him daily. In this chapter, we will consider the privilege of prayer, the importance of prayer, the power of prayer, and the process of prayer.

THE PRIVILEGE OF PRAYER

Many times, prayer is taken for granted, however it truly is a great privilege. Hebrews 4:14-16 gives us insight into the privilege of prayer.

Seeing then that we have a great High Priest who has passed through the heavens, Jesus the Son of God, let us hold fast our confession. For we do not have a High Priest who cannot sympathize with our weaknesses, but was in all points tempted as we are, yet without sin. Let us therefore come boldly to the

throne of grace, that we may obtain mercy and find
grace to help in time of need (Heb 4:14-16).

This text indicates three reasons one should count prayer a privilege. First, we see that prayer is a privilege because of the person
of our High Priest. Second, one should note that prayer is a privilege because of the practice of our High Priest. Third, we can see
that prayer is a privilege because of the access provided by our
High Priest.

The Person of our High Priest

Our High Priest is none other than God the Son, the second Person of the Trinity. He is Jesus Christ the Righteous, and it is in His
name that we enter into prayer. He has conquered sin, death, and
the grave. He has reentered the Throne Room of Heaven and He
has taken His seat at the right hand of the Father. When we pray in
the name of Jesus, we are coming into the presence of the Almighty
God. We enter the throne room of the Creator and Sustainer of the
Universe each time we say a prayer. Not only do we gain an audience with God, but we also have the privilege of approaching Him
as our loving Father. What an amazing privilege it is to commune
with the Father in the name of the Son, our High Priest.

The Practice of our High Priest

Our High Priest has made prayer a privilege not only because of
His Personhood, but also because of His Practice. The text points
out that we have a High Priest who can sympathize with us because

He truly understands what we face in this life. Jesus Himself was tempted in all points as we are, yet He never sinned. He understands what it is like to be tired, sad, happy, etc. He understands the struggles we face because He too became a man and faced the difficulties of this life. When we go to God in prayer, let us never forget that God understands exactly where we are. This truth is what allowed David to pray with honesty, from his heart, in the Psalms. This privilege is available to all who travel *Belief Way*.

The Access Provided by our High Priest

When we begin to understand the access that our High Priest has provided us, we begin to understand what a privilege prayer really is. Jesus not only provided access to a loving Heavenly Father, but He provided confident access. The text says to "come boldly to the throne of grace." Notice the phrase tells us how to come and where to come. We are to come "boldly." In other words, we can have confidence in our prayer. This confidence is based on where we are to come, i.e., "the throne of grace." Our confidence does not rest in ourselves, but in the grace of God applied to our lives through faith in Jesus and His finished work on the cross.

When Bill Clinton served as the President of the United States, my wife and I went to the White House. It was fun to take the tour and see part of the building. However, we were not allowed access to the President. As an American citizen, the President works for me, but I still did not have access to Him. Yet, there was a young lady that had access to him on a regular basis, almost at will. Her name is Chelsea. Throughout Bill Clinton's presidency she had full access to him because he was not only the

President, he was also her dad. I have access to the Infinite God and can come into His presence with boldness 24 hours a day, 7 days a week because Jesus, my High Priest, has paid the price to make me a child of God. I can call on Him at any moment calling out "Abba (Daddy), Father" (Gal 4:6). What a privilege prayer is! Prayer must be a priority stop on the road to Christian maturity.

The Importance of Prayer

Prayer must be a priority not only because it is a privilege, but also because it is important. By its very nature it can be observed that prayer is important to the growth of a Christian. This is true because of the injunction to pray, the examples of prayer, and the outcome of prayer.

The Injunction To Pray

Scripture gives a clear injunction to pray. The Old and New Testaments alike command us to spend time in prayer. The prophets, Jesus, and Paul all gave instruction to prayer. One such command can be found in 1 Thessalonians 5:17. The text simply reads, "pray without ceasing." Prayer is important to Christian growth because it is a clear command in Scripture.

The Examples of Prayer

Another indication of the importance of prayer has to do with the Biblical examples of its importance. The great leaders of the

Bible all took time to pray. Abraham spent time in prayer. David made prayer a high priority. Enoch "walked with God" (Gen 5:24) in prayer. Peter spent time in prayer. Paul prayed frequently. Jesus is our greatest example of prayer. If Jesus, God's Son, saw the need to make prayer a priority, we surely need to do so.

The Outcome of Prayer

The outcome of prayer is another reason that prayer is important. The Bible clearly teaches that God always answers the prayers of His children traveling down *Belief Way*. Sometimes the answer is exactly what we want. He says *yes*. Other times He answers with a *no*. It is in these times that prayer changes us, not our circumstances. Sometimes the Lord answers our prayers with *wait awhile*. However He answers, He always does answer and the outcome is for our good and His glory.

THE POWER OF PRAYER

The power of prayer is the third reason prayer must be a regular stop on our road to maturity. In the book of James it says, "the effective, fervent prayer of a righteous man avails much" (James 5:16b). James was writing to the early church. In the closing section of his letter he wanted to encourage the readers to make prayer a priority. In the paragraph where this sentence is found, James tells his readers to take every issue to the Lord in prayer. If one is suffering, he/she is to pray about it. If one is cheerful, he/she is to sing

Psalms. If one is sick, the answer is to pray in faith. If one has sin in his/her life, then a prayer of confession is in order.

He then makes the statement quoted above. The word *effective,* used in this context refers to sincerity. The word *fervent* refers to continually seeking the Lord until He answers. All those who are traveling *Belief Way* have had the righteousness of Christ applied to their lives. Thus, when a believer prays in sincerity, continually seeking God and His will, great things will happen.

James concludes the paragraph by reminding his readers of the example of Elijah. He was a human just like we are humans. He prayed and God did marvelous things through Him. First, he prayed and it did not rain in the land for 3 years. Then he prayed again, and the rain returned. Prayer is powerful and therefore prayer must be a priority for everyone traveling on *Belief Way*.

THE PROCESS OF PRAYER

Prayer must be a priority because prayer is a privilege, prayer is important, and there is power in prayer. Most believers would readily acknowledge the importance *of* prayer, but most spend very little time *in* prayer. One of the reasons individuals give for the lack of time spent in prayer is that they do not know how to pray.

On one occasion, one of Jesus' disciples felt the same way. After hearing Jesus pray, this disciple asked the Lord to teach him to pray. Jesus responded with the words we call the "Lord's Prayer." A better name for this text would be *the model prayer* because that is exactly what Jesus was doing. He was giving us a model to follow.

So he said to them, "When you pray, say: Our Father in heaven, Hallowed be Your name. Your kingdom come. Your will be done on earth as it is in Heaven. Give us day by day our daily bread. And forgive us our sins, for we also forgive everyone who is indebted to us. And do not lead us into temptation, but deliver us from the evil one (Luke 11:2-4).

This model includes praise, submission, petition, and confession. The Father is to be praised for who He is and what He does. We are to submit to His will. We can take any petition before Him. We can petition Him on behalf of our needs or the needs of others. Those needs might be physical, mental, emotional, or spiritual in nature. He hears and cares about all our petitions. We are to confess our sins, to seek His forgiveness and seek His help in forgiving others.

Scripture is full of examples of prayer, many of which are in the book of Psalms. David was always honest with God in his prayer life. When he was happy he praised and thanked the Lord in prayer. When he was fearful he looked to the Lord for help and strength. He even turned to the Lord when he was confused and angry. God was always there for David no matter what the circumstances. If you are traveling *Belief Way*, He will always be there for you as well.

Take a minute to stop and evaluate your prayer life. How are things going? Is prayer a priority stop as you travel the road to Christian maturity? What would the Lord say if He were asked about your prayer life? Take a minute and confess to Him where you have failed. Ask the Lord to help you to make prayer a regular stop on your journey to maturity.

Discussion Questions

1. What are three reasons that prayer must be a priority in the life of a believer?
2. In your opinion what is the greatest privilege of prayer?
3. List three reasons that prayer is important.
4. Give one Biblical example of the power of prayer.
5. Give one modern day example of the power of prayer.
6. Based on the model prayer that Jesus gave us, what four things should be included when we pray?
7. Which of these four are you most comfortable with?
8. Which of these four do you need to work on?

CHAPTER 4

Worship Must Be Worthy

Worship is an essential stop on the road to Christian maturity. While traveling *Belief Way* one must be sure worship is a routine event, because God deserves our worship and somehow, He uses worship to motivate and empowers us for personal growth and service. Most believers would agree that worship is important, but if asked to define worship a variety of answers would result. Not everything that passes as worship is pleasing to the Father and if it is not pleasing to our Lord, then it is not worthy to be called worship at all.

Worship may take various forms, but there are certain principles that are essential if worship is to be worthy. In order to ensure that our worship is worthy, this chapter will explore the *Object of Worship,* the *Attitude of Worship,* and the *Act of Worship.* Though many texts of Scripture could be considered, this study will concentrate on Revelation 4-5. In these chapters we gain a glimpse of a future time of worshiping the Lord in Heaven. Examining these passages will enable us to draw some principles essential to all worship experiences. At the conclusion of the chapter there will also be a brief consideration of various *Aids of Worship.*

THE OBJECT OF WORSHIP

God the Father

> Immediately I was in the Spirit; and behold, a throne set in heaven, and One that sat on the throne. And He who sat there was like a jasper and a sardius stone in appearance and there was a rainbow around the throne, in appearance like an emerald (Rev 4:2-3).

God is to be the object of all worship. He is worthy of all honor, glory, and praise because of who He is and because of what He does. Throughout Scripture, Old Testament and New Testament alike, God alone is worthy of worship. When people attempted to worship angels, idols, nature, other men, or any created thing they were corrected. Worship is reserved for the One True God and Him alone.

When we speak of God as revealed in the Bible, we speak of the Trinity. We understand that there is only one God yet three distinct persons, i.e. the Father, the Son, and the Holy Spirit. Each Person of the Trinity is God, and each Person of the Trinity is worthy of our worship in general. However, in Scripture the focus of worship is usually placed on the Father and the Son while the Spirit motivates, empowers, and aids us in worship. He always points us to Jesus, Who has opened the door of access to the Father.

This is the picture of Worship that we find in Revelation 4-5. Chapter four begins with John indicating that he was in the Spirit when he saw the heavenly vision of these two chapters. The Spirit gave John a glimpse of perfect worship which no doubt affected the way John himself approached his personal worship experiences the rest of his life. In chapter four, John revealed the worship of the Father and in chapter five the worship of the Son.

Chapter 4 verses 2-3 gives us a view of the Father. Verse 2 indicates His position when it states that He is on a throne in Heaven. The Father is the Almighty Ruler of all Creation; His throne is set in the Heaven of heavens; He is the Creator and Sustainer of all that is. Having established the position of the Father, verse 3 gives a further description of the One on the Throne.

The Father is described as being like a jasper and a sardius stone in His appearance. The jasper was a clear stone and obviously represents His purity. The Father is pure and there is no shadow of turning with Him. He cannot be tempted by, nor does He tempt anyone else to sin. The sardius was red like a ruby and is a constant reminder of the sacrifice He made in giving His Son for the salvation of mankind. The verse goes on to explain that around the throne is a rainbow that was like an emerald. The rainbow serves as a constant reminder that the Father is One who is always faithful to keep His Word. Truly the Father is worthy of worship because of who He is and what He does.

God the Son

But one of the elders said to me, "do not weep. Behold, the Lion of the tribe of Judah, the Root of David, has

prevailed to open the scroll and to loose its seven seals."
And I looked, and behold, in the midst of the throne
and of the four living creatures, and in the midst of the
elders, stood a Lamb as though it had been slain, having seven horns and seven eyes, which are the seven
spirits of God sent out into all the earth (Rev 5:5-6).

In chapter 5, John noticed a scroll in the Father's hand and a
voice was heard seeking for someone worthy to open the scroll.
No one was found and thus John began to weep. John's attention
was quickly directed to the only One worthy to open the scroll, to
Jesus the Son. Verses 5 and 6 give a brief description of the Son,
which indicates that He too is worthy of worship.

One of the elders standing near John began a verbal description of the Son in verse five. He told John that the Son was "the
Lion of the tribe of Judah" and "the root of David." In verse six,
John looked to see this One who is worthy and must have been
shocked by the site. This "Lion" is described as a "Lamb" that had
been slain. However, the "Lamb" had seven horns and seven eyes.
The titles, the horns, and the eyes all indicate who Jesus is. The
picture of a slain lamb indicates what He has done on our behalf.

The Titles

The two titles given are messianic titles that point to the reality that
Jesus is the infinite God-Man. He is the only mediator between the
Father and mankind. At the time of John's writing, horns were rep-
resentative of deity, the eyes indicate knowledge, and the number
seven in Scripture always represents completeness. Thus, the pic-

ture given indicates that the Lamb is the Messiah, the embodiment of complete deity and knowledge. He is in His very essence God.

The Slain Lamb

The imagery of the slain lamb indicates the sacrifice Jesus made on our behalf. This One who is the Messiah, perfect God, with perfect knowledge, gave Himself as a sacrifice for you. Though perfect, He died upon a cruel cross in our place taking the penalty for our sin, conquering sin, death, and the grave. He rose again three days later, ascended to Heaven, sat down at the right hand of the Father and now offers forgiveness of sin and a new relationship with God to those who will place their faith in Him. Without a doubt, Jesus is worthy of worship not only because of what He has done but also because of who He is.

In general, the object of our worship is God, this would include the Father, the Son, and the Spirit. However, the main focus of our worship rests with the Father and the Son. The Spirit motivates, empowers, and aids us in the act of worship. He also works in our lives to enable us to approach the act of worship with the proper attitude.

THE ATTITUDE OF WORSHIP

Around the throne were twenty-four thrones, and on the thrones I saw twenty-four elders sitting, clothed in white robes; and they had crowns of gold on their heads...The twenty-four elders fall down before

Him who sits on the throne and worship Him who lives forever and ever, and cast their crowns before the throne...Now when He had taken the scroll, the four living creatures and the twenty-four elders fell down before the Lamb, each having a harp, and golden bowls full of incense, which are the prayers of the saints (Rev 4:4, 10; 5:8).

The Attitude of Worship toward the Father

In chapter 4, we find the elders, which represents all the saved of all times, worshipping the Father. Verse 10 indicates that when they worship, the elders bow down before the Father and cast their crowns before His throne. This action speaks to the proper attitude of worship. The act of bowing down before Him indicates submission and reverence. Submission is always present in true worship. Worship acknowledges that God is God, and we are His creation. Therefore, we revere and submit to Him.

The casting of the crowns reveals another important attitude of worship. By this act, the elders acknowledge their own dependence upon the Father. Scripture indicates that the crowns are rewards for service to the Lord while on earth. This act is an admission that apart from God's grace, mercy, and empowerment the crowns would not have been received to begin with. All honor, glory, and praise belong to God.

The Attitude of Worship toward the Son

The focus of the elders' worship shifts from the Father to the Son in chapter 5, but the attitude of worship remains the same. In verse 8, we find the elders bowing down before the Lamb in this same attitude of submission and reverence. Whether the focus is the Father or the Son, whether the worship is accomplished through music or through the spoken word, the attitude of true worship is always an attitude of submission, reverence, and dependence upon our Living Lord.

THE ACT OF WORSHIP

Holy, holy, holy, Lord God Almighty, Who was and is and is to come! (Rev 4:8)

You are worthy, O Lord, to receive glory and honor and power; for You created all things, and by Your will they exist and were created (Rev 5:11).

You are worthy to take the scroll, and to open its seals; for You were slain, and have redeemed us to God by Your blood out of every tribe and tongue and people and nation, And made us kings and priests to our God; and we shall reign on the earth (Rev 5:9).

Worthy is the Lamb that was slain to receive power and riches and wisdom, and strength and honor and glory and blessing! (Rev 5:12)

Blessing and honor and glory and power be to Him who sits on the throne, and to the Lamb, forever and ever! (Rev 5:13)

The Act of Worshiping the Father

In chapter 4, the Father is worshipped first by the living creatures around the throne (verse 8) and then by the elders (verse 11). In both instances we find that the words are spoken in unison. Through the spoken word the Father is worshipped both for who He is and for what He has done. He is the "Lord God Almighty..." and He "created all things." We too should praise the Father through the spoken word. We should praise Him for who He is and for what He does.

The Act of Worshiping the Son

In chapter 5, we see the Son worshiped by the living creatures, the elders, and then by all of creation. The worship here seems to be accomplished through song and through prayer. The elders have harps and bowls representing the prayers of the saints. Verse 9 indicates that they sang a new song. In verse 12 it seems that the worship was accomplished through speaking loudly. Like the Father, the Lamb was worshipped both for who He is and for what He has done.

In verse 13, we find all of creation joins in the glorious scene. The worship is focused on both the Father and the Son. All of creation must take its rightful place and acknowledge that God is God and man is man. Finally, every knee bows in worship of both the Father and the Son. Some worship out of love and some out of necessity, but all worship.

Worship Now

Those traveling *Belief Way* do not have to wait to worship the Lord; we can do it today. In fact, if one is to grow towards Christian maturity, regular worship is essential. Worthy worship must be focused in the right direction, must be approached with the right attitude, and must be accomplished as a specific act of worshiping God for who He is and what He has done.

The Setting of Worship

The act of worship should be accomplished in two settings, each of which is important to proper Christian growth. One must be involved in regular public worship of the Father and Son with others traveling on Belief Way. However, if the only worship experienced is public worship, growth will be hindered. Private worship is also an important part of the Christian experience. Attention will now focus on a brief consideration of each of these important settings of worship.

Public Worship

Public worship is accomplished when the church meets together. There are certain aspects of public worship that are essential and have been practiced in both the Old and New Testaments. Public worship is accomplished through prayer, music, song, testimony, giving, and preaching of the Word. When we pray, worship should be a major focus. Music played and songs sung should bring honor and glory to the Lord. Testimonies of God's faithfulness should be a part of our public worship. Throughout Scripture, giving is seen as an act of worship towards our loving Lord who supplies all our needs. The preaching of God's Word is part of our worship experience as well as our response to the preaching of the Word.

Private Worship

Just as a child cannot grow properly if they only eat once a week, so one traveling *Belief Way* is unable to grow properly if worship is only experienced in a public setting once a week. Worship needs to become a part of our daily lives. We must set aside time not only to read the Bible and pray, but some time should be spent each day in Worship of our Lord. We can worship Him through prayer and song daily. We should mature to the point that we live in an attitude of worship, constantly submitting to God in humble reverence and acknowledging our dependence on Him.

My son, Ben, loves to listen to worship music. He has special needs that prevent him from singing. However, that does not stop him from worshiping the Lord through music. When he first comes out of his room in the morning, he wants Christian music playing throughout the house. When we get in the truck to go to work, the store, or take a long a trip, Ben wants worship music playing. When he lays down at night, his cd player rings forth with music praising God for who He is and what He does. May we all learn to love worship like Ben!

The Aids to Worship

As already noted, our greatest aid to worship is the Holy Spirit Himself. He is our Helper and Guide; He motivates and empowers us to truly worship God. There are several practical aids that He can use to help us in our worship. These are listed below:

1. Scripture – repeating words of praise directly to God (The Psalms are great for this.)
2. Hymns – singing or reading words of hymns that ascribe praise
3. Contemporary Songs – singing or reading words of newer songs that ascribe praise
4. Music – playing music unto the Lord
5. Books – reading books that teach us more about worship
6. Poems – writing, reading, and quoting poems that ascribe praise
7. Prayer – Talking to the Lord in terms of praise and thanksgiving

Discussion Questions

1. Who should be the object of our Worship?
2. What role does the Holy Spirit play in Worship?
3. What attitudes are essential for us as we approach Worship?
4. What two settings of Worship should we be involved in?

5. Which of these two settings do you find easiest to participate in?
6. What is your favorite aid to Worship?
7. What area of Worship needs the most work in your life?

CHAPTER 5

Fellowship is Fundamental

I have always been one to enjoy travel whether it is by land, sea, or air. It has always been a personal goal to see every state in the U.S. and as many foreign countries as possible. It has been my privilege to visit 49 US states and five foreign countries. Travel is usually very relaxing, exciting, and enjoyable to this author. Though I enjoy travel just for the sake of traveling, it is always more enjoyable when traveling with others. It is a special joy for me to travel with Cindy, Ben, other family members, and friends. Travel shared is more enjoyable than traveling alone.

The same is true for the person traveling *Belief Way*. The fact that an individual on *Belief Way* always has the Lord as a companion on the road to Christian Maturity and the Eternal Home is exciting enough. However, the Lord designed *Belief Way* to be traveled with other believers. As one is on this magnificent journey, the joy is compounded when the journey is shared through true Christian fellowship. In fact, *Fellowship is Fundamental* to proper Christian growth.

This chapter will explore Christian fellowship by considering its root, its reason, its requirements, and its results. In the first section we will discuss the definition of the word translated "fellowship" in the New Testament. In the second section attention will be given to the reason we can experience this fellowship. There are certain requirements to enter into and maintain Christian fellowship; these will be examined in the third section. The final section of this chapter will concentrate on some of the results of fellowship.

THE ROOT OF FELLOWSHIP

The word *fellowship* is found 14 times in the New Testament, 12 of which are a translation of the Greek word, "koinonia". One is a translation of a derivative of "koinonia" and the other is an entirely different word. Of the thirteen times "koinonia" is thus translated, two are prescriptive while the other instances are descriptive. In 1 Corinthians 10:20 we are told not to have "koinonia" with demons and in Ephesians 5:11 the reader is commanded not to have "koinonia" with the "unfruitful works of darkness." In the other eleven passages, we find "koinonia" used as a descriptive characteristic that is the result of some action.

The word "koinonia" carries with it several ideas that must be understood in order to grasp what is meant by the translation, "fellowship." Included in the idea of "fellowship" are association, community, joint participation, partnership, and intimacy. For individuals to have "koinonia" there must be an association; however, an association alone does not mean there is true fellowship.

Community is an important aspect of "koinonia" that refers to the idea of an extended family or support system as seen in Acts 2:42. This support does not flow in only one direction but requires mutual participation, a partnership mentality like we see in Philippians 1:5 and Galatians 2:9.

Intimacy is an additional part of "koinonia" and refers to the fact that the partnership is more than a surface relationship as we see in 1 John 1:7.[5] Thus, when we read the word *fellowship* in the New Testament we are talking about an association of two or more individuals that are part of a community support system where each member is a full partner, operating through mutual participation in a growing intimate relationship.

THE REASON FOR FELLOWSHIP

Since the beginning of my journey on *Belief Way* it has been my privilege to visit and preach in many congregations throughout this country and I am always amazed by the immediate sense of fellowship that has greeted me in most of these visits. The various congregations have been diverse in background, culture, worship style, etc. but the sense of Christian fellowship has been ever present. How is it that a young man from Colorado can experience an immediate sense of fellowship with people he never met before in places as different as Texas and Massachusetts, Virginia and New Hampshire? How is it that the same person could experience this immediate sense of connection with congregations from various ethnicities and cultures including: Spanish, Portuguese, Nepali, African American, Slavic, Creole, Haitian, and Canadian congregations? It is because of two main areas of commonality; we have the same faith and the same family.

Our Common Faith

In 1 Corinthians 1:9 this fellowship is referred to as "the fellowship of Jesus"; in Philippians 2:1 it is referred to as the "fellowship of the Spirit" and in 1 John 1:3 we find that fellowship with one another is based upon fellowship with the Father and the Son. All those who have placed their faith in Jesus and entered into fellowship with the Father, Son, and Holy Spirit have a supernatural fellowship with one another that transcends culture, economics, personality, and any other normal barriers to friendship. Our common faith is the first reason that we can have fellowship with one another.

Our Common Family

Growing up as the youngest of nine children was an exciting opportunity. There were times of joy and times of sorrow. As one could expect there were times of discussion, argument, and even fighting. However, one thing I learned early on was that family sticks together. We may fuss and fight at times, but love was unquestioned and when things got tough, we were there for each other. Why? Because we were family. So it is with those who are part of God's family.

When a person trusts Jesus as his/her Savior and begins his/her journey on *Belief Way*, he/she is born into *God's Forever Family*. We now have God Himself as their Heavenly Father and all believers as brothers and sisters. Whenever I have gone to a new church it was like meeting long lost family members for the first time. Fellowship was sensed immediately in most congregations of which I have attended. In fact, every church I have visited I have sensed true Christian Fellowship on some level. The level of fellowship experienced is directly related to how I and those of that congregation were meeting the requirements for fellowship.

THE REQUIREMENTS OF FELLOWSHIP

When one considers the requirements for fellowship there are two basic areas to examine. The first consideration has to do with the requirements of gaining fellowship and the second concept to explore is the requirements of maintaining fellowship. Before one can experience true Christian fellowship, he/she must have experienced salvation and must be walking in the light. To maintain this fellowship, one must continue to walk in the light while exhibiting love, grace, and forgiveness.

Gaining Fellowship

The first requirement to have Christian fellowship is to be a Christian. It was noted earlier that this fellowship is directly connected to fellowship with the Father through Jesus the Son. Fellowship with other believers is a by-product of fellowship with God and fellowship with God is only available through Jesus. The

Holy Spirit affects that fellowship as He works in the individual lives of those He indwells, and He indwells all those who have trusted their lives and their eternity to Jesus.

It is not however, a given that all Christians have fellowship with one another. The fact is that it is possible for two believers who worship in the same congregation to go through life without ever being in fellowship with one another. 1 John 1:6-7 teaches us that we must walk in the light if we are to have fellowship with one another. In order for one to walk in the light he must not only have come to the place of salvation but must also be living a life of obedience to the Lord. When we walk in the light, we have true fellowship with God and with other believers.

Maintaining Fellowship

The day I was born into the Ballard family I had an immediate relationship with my parents, brothers, sisters, and a large extended family. The problem is that these relationships have been strained from time to time. I really did not do anything to begin these relationships, but I have to work to maintain them. The same is true with Christian fellowship. The minute I trusted my life into Jesus' hands I was born into His family, began to walk in the light, and had fellowship with other believers. However, I must be sure to maintain that fellowship.

I know that I need to "walk in the light." In the text mentioned earlier, 1 John 1:7, the Greek word translated *walk* is in the present tense and carries with it the idea of continuous action. In other words, the verse is stating that if we want to have fellowship with one another we must continuously "walk in the light." Thus, we must be constantly concerned about living in obedience to our Lord in every area of our lives. When we fall short, we must confess our sin and seek God's help to get back on track.

Three Crucial Acts of Obedience

There are three areas of obedience that are extremely important to maintaining fellowship. We are commanded to deal with one another in love, grace, and forgiveness. If we fail to do so we are not "walking in the light" and cannot expect to experience Christian fellowship. Jesus told us to "...love one another; as I have loved you" (John 13:34). This kind of love is an unconditional love that always seeks what is best for the one loved. In His love the Father deals with us by grace, giving us blessings which we do not deserve. In the same way we are to treat one another with this same kind of grace. Forgiveness is also a necessary element to maintaining fellowship. We are all human and we all fail, letting each other down from time to time. We must be quick to forgive even as the Father is quick to forgive us.

If we want to experience true fellowship, we must come to faith in Jesus Christ and began to "walk in the light" by living a life of obedience to Him. If we want to maintain that fellowship, we must continue to live obedient to our Lord. We must also make love, grace, and forgiveness priorities in our relationships with other believers. As we walk in the light exhibiting these characteristics, we will experience true Christian fellowship and continue our journey on *Belief Way*.

THE RESULTS OF FELLOWSHIP

Everything we do causes some kind of result including fellowship. When we engage in true fellowship there are several results that we can expect to occur. We will concentrate on the following three: *Mutual Encouragement, Mutual Accountability, and Mutual Growth.*

Mutual Encouragement

Everyone who travels *Belief Way* experiences times of joy and times of sorrow. At times it seems like everything is going great and life couldn't be better. Other times life gets difficult, and we seem to lose hope. When we are involved in fellowship, we are part of a support system where we have built in encouragement to enjoy the good times and make it through the difficult times. When one member of our fellowship group rejoices, we all rejoice together. When one member of our group hurts, we hurt together. Today I might provide the encouragement, but next week I may need the encouragement of others. Either way I am a mutual participant in this wonderful experience.

Mutual Accountability

When traveling on *Belief Way* there are many things on the side of the road that try to distract us and divert our attention away from growth. At times we all can be easily distracted, but if we are involved in true fellowship we have a support system where we experience mutual accountability. When we see a brother or sister in Christ getting off track, we encourage him/her in love.

We encourage him/her to seek the Lord's forgiveness and to get back on the road to maturity.

Mutual Growth

As we continue in this experience of Christian fellowship we grow personally. Together we grow closer to the Lord and closer to one another. We grow by encouraging others and by being encouraged. We grow by being held accountable and holding one another accountable. In other words, the mere fact that we are traveling *Belief Way* in fellowship with other believers causes us to get further on the road to Christian Maturity, faster than would be possible if we were traveling alone.

DISCUSSION QUESTIONS

1. What is the main Greek word that is translated "fellowship" and how many times is it used in the New Testament?
2. There are five important aspects of fellowship, what are they, which one do you feel is most important, and why?
3. What are the two requirements to have fellowship?
4. What is required to maintain that fellowship?
5. Name and discuss three areas of obedience that are particularly important to maintain fellowship with other believers.
6. Name and discuss three results of experiencing true Christian fellowship.

CHAPTER 6

Evangelism Is Essential

While living in North Carolina, my wife and I made our first trip to Washington D.C. We had a great time. The event was truly exciting to us both. It was a great privilege to see the Capital City. When we arrived back in North Carolina, we were so excited about the experience that we just had to tell everybody how much we enjoyed the trip.

A couple of years after that first visit to the Capital, we moved to Deerfield, VA and were less than three hours from D.C. Living where we did, we were able to see the Capital much more often. The more experience we had with the city, the more information we gave folks when discussing Washington D.C. with them. Whenever we had the opportunity, we would encourage people to make the trip and always suggest certain sites they would not want to miss. Why? Because we had experienced the excitement and we wanted others to do so as well.

When a person begins their journey on *Belief Way* it is normal for them to share their excitement with others. They want family, friends, associates, acquaintances, and even strangers to experience this newfound peace and joy. As one shares the Good News of Jesus, he/she not only helps others come to personal faith in Christ, but also experiences personal growth. In fact, if one does not share one's faith with others at least one means of growth is missing from his/her journey. In other words, sharing the faith is an essential part of growing as a Christian.

The word "evangelism" means to proclaim the good news. Within the context of Biblical Christianity, it means: to tell others about the good news that though we are all sinners and deserve death; Jesus loves us; died on the cross in our place; rose again conquering sin and death; will forgive us of our sin; and give us a home in heaven, if we trust our lives to Him. Evangelism is essential to our growth personally and to the growth of God's family. Thus, in this chapter we will consider the Mandate of Evangelism, the Motivation for Evangelism, the Methods of Evangelism, and the Movement towards Evangelism.

THE MANDATE OF EVANGELISM

As Jesus began His Ministry here on earth, He began by calling two men to follow Him. The account of their call is recorded for us in Matthew 4:18. *"Then He said to them, 'Follow Me, and I will make you fishers of men.'"* Jesus knew that He had 3 ½ years to prepare His followers to lead the church that would change the world forever. They needed to grow and part of that growth was for them to become "fishers of men." For one to be a "fisher of men" he/she must tell others about Jesus and lead them to trust their lives to Him.

Throughout His earthly ministry Jesus continued to teach His followers the importance of evangelism. They learned of its importance by His example; evangelism was His priority so it must be the priority of His followers as well. They also learned by His teaching. On several occasions He told His followers that they must share Him with others. On occasion He even sent them out in pairs to share the Good News.

At the conclusion of Jesus' earthly ministry, He commanded His followers to make evangelism a priority in their lives. In fact, every Gospel writer includes in his account of Jesus' last hours on earth His command to share the Gospel. Matthew's account is the most detailed and most well-known. It is found in Matthew 28:18-20.

> And Jesus came and spoke to them, saying, All authority has been given to me in heaven and on earth. Go therefore and make disciples of all the nations, baptizing them in the name of the Father and of the Son and of the Holy Spirit, teaching them to observe all things that I have commanded you; and lo, I am with you always, even to the end of the age.' Amen.

We refer to this passage of Scripture as "The Great Commission" because it is Jesus' commission and command to all His followers. This was His command to His followers in the first century and to His followers in the twenty-first century. The command speaks of Jesus' power, His plan, and His promise. He began by reminding the early disciples that He has the power or authority to command His followers. He then issued the command by giving His plan. Jesus' followers are to 1. Make disciples of all nations, 2. Baptize them in the Name of the Father, Son, and Holy Spirit, and 3. Teach them to observe all things He has commanded them. He concluded His commission by issuing His followers a promise. The promise is that He would always be with them as they share the gospel, even to the end of the world.

The Gospel of Mark is the shortest of the four and the least detailed. Yet even Mark included Jesus' command to evangelize. It is found in Mark 16:15: *"Go into all the world and proclaim the gospel to every creature."* Mark is short, sweet, and to the point. The command is to proclaim the good news of Jesus to everyone.

Luke wrote two books of the New Testament that go together. The Gospel of Luke is part one and the book of Acts is part two. Luke waited to record the last events of Jesus' time on earth until the first chapter of Acts. The last words of Jesus on earth that Luke recorded are found in Acts 1:8.

> But you shall receive power when the Holy Spirit has come upon you; and you shall be witnesses to Me in Jerusalem, and in all Judea and Samaria, and to the end of the earth.

In this verse Jesus promised His followers that the Holy Spirit would empower them to be witnesses for Him. He also gave them a plan to follow. The followers were to begin in their own town, move out to the neighboring areas, and ultimately to the end of the earth. Wherever they went, they were to witness to others about Jesus. The followers of Jesus today are to continue to follow this plan. We are to rely on the Spirit to empower us. Then we must act in that power, witnessing to those around us, and even taking the message to the very ends of the earth.

John's Gospel is much different than the other three. He wrote several years after the others, he included several details the others failed to mention, and he left out some details they had already shared. Yet, John also records Jesus' command to evangelize. In the final earthly event that John records, Jesus is in the process of restoring Peter after his failure. The account is recorded in John 21:15-25. Three times in this text Jesus asked Peter the following question: *"Do you love Me?"* After Peter answered the question the first time Jesus told Him, *"Feed My lambs."* The second time Jesus said, *"Tend My sheep."* The third time He said, *Feed My sheep."* Each command refers to the Great Commission. If Peter loved the Lord he was to evangelize, baptize, and teach others.

At the beginning of His earthly ministry, Jesus commanded His followers to make evangelism a priority. During His 3½ years of earthly ministry He continued to emphasize the importance of all His followers participating in evangelism. At the conclusion of His earthly ministry, He commanded his followers to share the good news of salvation with the entire world. There is no doubt that if one is a follower of Jesus, he/she lives under His mandate to evangelize the world.

THE MOTIVATION FOR EVANGELISM

What motivates those traveling *Belief Way* to make evangelism a priority? There are several issues involved in evangelistic motivation. In this part of the chapter, I would like to suggest three factors that should motivate every believer to be involved in sharing the Good News with others. The first factor to consider is simply *obedience*. The second factor is *love for our Lord*. The third factor we will consider is *love for others*.

Obedience

When one begins their journey on *Belief Way* he/she is beginning a new life. This life is a life of submission to the Lord of Lords. We are now obligated to live a life that is pleasing to Him. He not only created us, but He also purchased us from the slave block of sin. 1 Corinthians 6:20 reminds us of this fact. *"For you were bought at a price; therefore glorify God in your body and in your spirit, which are Gods."* You see, the fact is we belong to Him. Therefore, we are obligated to live a life of obedience to the Lord and as seen earlier, He has commanded His followers to share the Good News. However, obedience is not the only motivating factor.

Love For God

The Bible teaches us that we love God because He first loved us. How could we not love the One who gave His all for us? When we first come to faith in God we have a love for Him that begins to grow. As time passes and we come to know Him better, our love grows stronger. As one grows in love with the Lord, His desires become our desires, and His priorities become our priorities.

In 1 Peter 3:9 the Bible says that the Lord is *"..not willing that any should perish but that all should come to repentance."* If we love God it will be our desire to see "all…come to repentance" as well. As one grows in his love for the Lord, he will be motivated to share Jesus with others. In addition, we will find that as our love for God grows, so will our love for others.

Love For Others

On one occasion during Jesus' earthly ministry, He was asked what the greatest commandment is. His response is found in Matthew 22:37-40.

> Jesus said to him, "'You shall love the LORD your God with all your heart, with all your soul, and with all your mind.' This is the first and great commandment. And the second is like it: 'You shall love your neighbor as yourself.' On these two commandments hang all the Law and the Prophets."

Not only are we to love God, but we are to love others as well. In fact, Jesus even taught that we are to love our enemies. Now if we truly love someone then we want what is best for that person. If we believe that God is Holy and man is a sinner; that Heaven is real and Hell is real; that man cannot save himself and that faith in Jesus is the only way one can have eternal life; and if we love others, then we must share the Good News of Jesus with them. We cannot truly love someone and not care about his or her eternal destination. If we had a family member, friend, neighbor, work associate, or just an acquaintance that had some debilitating disease and then we heard about a new treatment, we would rush over and tell them the Good News. Every human has sin, and the consequences are eternal. If you are traveling through life on *Belief Way* you have the remedy. JUST SHARE IT!

THE METHODS OF EVANGELISM

Having established the importance of evangelism the question that arises is, "How does one accomplish evangelism?" There are two primary ways to communicate the Gospel: Pulpit Evangelism and Personal Evangelism. Pulpit Evangelism refers to the public preaching of the Gospel within the context of a worship service. Personal Evangelism refers to believers sharing the Good News of Jesus, outside of the worship setting.

A man was once asked, "How do you share the Gospel?" He answered, "Any way I can!" The fact is there are hundreds, if not thousands of methods Christians use to accomplish the task of sharing the Gospel with others. However, all the methods out there end up falling into one of three general categories: Lifestyle Evangelism, Media Evangelism, and Verbal Evangelism.

Lifestyle Evangelism

This method of evangelism says that I will be a witness to those around me by the way I live my life. People are watching Christians and they see how we act and react. The idea is, when people see the difference in how a Christian lives compared to a non-Christian, they will come to faith in Christ. It is often said, "actions speak louder than words."

Without a doubt it is essential for believers to live a life that shows the world that we are different. There are certain things a Christian should not do that others may do and there are certain things a Christian should do that others may not. Those who see us on a daily basis should be able to observe that we handle times of trial and stress different than others. There are many ways we can show the world that Jesus has made a difference in our lives.

Yet, it is important to note that observing someone's example alone cannot make one a Christian. An individual can observe a believer for years and even note that there is something different about that person. In fact, he could even desire to have whatever it is that makes the believer act and react the way he does, but that still does not bring new life to the observer. There must come a point in time where the observer is confronted with the truth of the Gospel message and he must trust his life to Jesus personally. This requires more than simply living a "good Christian life." It requires a confrontation with the Gospel.

Media Evangelism

A popular form of evangelism today is what I would call media evangelism. This category would include things like tracts, magazines, books, radio, videos, etc. Sometimes we do not have an opportunity to sit down and share the Gospel with someone, but we can give out a tract, magazine, or a book that shares the Gospel. Believers can also use radio, television, and the internet to share the Gospel.

There are several advantages to using various forms of media to present the Gospel. First, it does not require much skill from the person who introduces another individual to the Gospel with these methods. All one has to do is give out a tract or a book, suggest a radio station or a web page, etc. A second advantage is that the use of media seems less threatening to the target audience. If someone is listening to the radio and hears a commercial that presents the Gospel, they don't have to listen if they choose to ignore the message. However, if they want more information, a method of contact is usually provided. A third advantage is that once a web page is set up or a tract or book is printed you do not have to worry about leaving anything out while attempting to share. All you do is introduce people to the information and let them examine it for themselves.

Verbal Evangelism

Verbal Evangelism is the method that Jesus advocated and used Himself. For someone to believe, they must hear the Good News of Jesus. We must open our mouths and share the Gospel with others. Remember the last words of Jesus recorded by each of the Gospel writers. The idea conveyed by each was that of speaking to others about Jesus. Every true believer has the ability to share with others how to begin traveling on *Belief Way*. All one has to do is be *a witness*.

What is *a witness* anyway? A *witness* is someone who re-counts what they have experienced. If you were standing on the street corner at the time of a car accident you would most likely be interviewed by a police officer and you might even have to appear in court. If you went to court you would be required to be *a witness*. What does that mean? It means that you tell what you saw, heard, felt, etc. The same is true when you tell others about how they can begin traveling on *Belief Way*. All you have to do is tell them what happened to you.

The Apostle Paul shared his personal testimony of salvation on several occasions in the New Testament. Each time he followed a certain outline that helped him be a good witness. We can see the outline in Acts 26:1-23. This outline is a good example for any believer to follow. First, Paul spoke of his life before he came to know Christ. Second, he spoke of how he came to know Christ. Third, he spoke of his life since he came to faith in Jesus.

The exciting thing about this outline is that it can be used in so many ways. I use this same outline for a 60-second testimony, for an introduction to the Gospel, and for a detailed testimony that might last several minutes. Take a minute to read the following example of a 60-second testimony.

> You know, I used to worry about death. I wondered what would happen if someone I loved were to die. I thought how could I live without ever seeing my loved one again. Then I met Jesus. I came to realize that death was a result of sin and everyone has sinned. I also came to understand that Jesus loved me and died in my place so that I could be forgiven of my sin. I learned that if I would trust my life into His hands He would forgive me of my sin and give me a home in Heaven. Right then I trusted my life to Jesus.

Since trusting Jesus and receiving His free gift of eternal life, I have found a new peace concerning death. I learned that the key is for me to help my loved ones trust Jesus as well. Then I can have the assurance that even if my loved ones die, or if I die, we will see each other again when we get to heaven.

Stop a minute and use the following outline to work on your 60-second testimony.

My Life Before Christ

_____

_____

_____

_____

_____

_____

_____

How I Came to Christ

_____

_____

_____

_____

_____

_____

_____

My Life Since Trusting Christ

_____

_____

_____

_____

_____

_____

_____

_____

In addition to sharing your testimony there are hundreds of programs out there that are designed to help believers learn how to evangelize their world. Many people have developed their own personal method of sharing their faith with others as well. It is always good to ask your pastor or Bible Study teacher about how you can learn more ways to share the Gospel. There are a few key ingredients that should be included in any Gospel presentation. The essentials include: *1. Eternal Life (Heaven) is a free Gift. 2. Every human has sinned. 3. No one can save himself/herself. 4. God is Holy and Just, therefore He must punish sin. 5. God is love and does not want to punish us. 6. Jesus died in our place taking the penalty for our sin and He rose again, defeating sin, death, and the grave. 7. You must repent of your sin and trust your life Jesus. Then He will give you His free gift of eternal life.*

THE MOVEMENT TOWARDS EVANGELISM

It is great to know that God expects all Believers to be involved in personal evangelism. It is wonderful to feel motivated to start evangelizing others around you. It is exciting to know how to evangelize. However, until you actually start evangelizing, you are not yet fulfilling God's plan of growth for your life.

One must make a distinct effort to share his or her faith with others. Once I met a man who took his watch and painted a red dot on the 4. He said the reason for the dot was to remind him each day that if he had not shared the Gospel with someone by 4:00 in the afternoon, time was running out for the day. When 4:00 came if he had not yet attempted to tell someone about Jesus my friend would stop what he was doing, and go find someone to share with. Every believer needs to hold himself/herself accountable for sharing the Gospel on a regular basis. We must move from merely talking about evangelism to actually doing evangelism.

Many times this movement requires some help from another Christian friend. Find someone who shares their faith on a regular basis and ask them to help you to grow in this area. The best way to make this move is to take some OJT, that's On the Job Training. Ask someone like a pastor, teacher, or just a good Christian friend to take you with him or her when they share Jesus with others. You will learn by observing.

As we continue to travel on *Belief Way* we will find that if we want to grow towards Christian Maturity we must share Jesus with others. As we lead others to faith in Him, we will actually grow in our own faith. Personal Evangelism is truly essential to spiritual growth.

Discussion Questions

1. During what part of Jesus' ministry did He teach His followers to evangelize?
2. What are two ways Jesus taught His followers to evangelize?
3. How many of the Gospel writers included Jesus' command to share the Gospel?
4. What three factors should motivate the Believer to evangelize?
5. What are the three general categories of personal evangelism?
6. Do you know someone who needs to hear your testimony? Who?
7. Do you have a plan to move from talking about evangelism to doing evangelism?

CHAPTER 7

Ministry Is a Mandate

When I was growing up, I could not wait for the opportunity to drive, travel, and see this great nation. Because of my desire to learn all I could about driving I paid close attention to almost everything my Dad did when he was in the driver's seat. After watching him for a while, I began to ask questions so I could learn all I needed to be a good driver.

One of the things I learned early on was the way my Dad watched out for other people on the road. Whether traveling a familiar street in our hometown or some unfamiliar highway, if Dad noticed another driver on the side of the road with car problems, he stopped to help. Sometimes, they needed something simple like gas, a jumpstart, a little push, etc. Sometimes they needed extensive auto care. Whatever the need, my Dad would help if at all possible.

I remember asking Dad a few times why he helped people he did not even know. He told me he did it because Jesus wanted us to and besides, one day he might be the one who needed the help.

You know, life is like that. Sometimes we are there to lend a helping hand to others and sometimes we are in need of a helping hand.

As we travel *Belief Way* we are to help others traveling with us. The help may come in the form of instruction, service, encouragement, a listening ear, or in several other ways. As we give this help, we are being obedient to our Lord, and we are growing in our walk with Him. It is amazing how when we take time to help others in their growth as a Christian, we end up growing ourselves. In addition, we will find that while we can be there to minister to others, Sometimes we need others to minister to us.

This chapter will talk about this process of ministry. We will consider two main topics relating to our mandate of ministry. First, we will look at the Call to Ministry. Second, we will consider the Conduct of Ministry.

THE CALL TO MINISTRY

What is "the call to ministry"? Who is called to ministry? How do I know if I am called to ministry? These are questions that every growing Christian will face at one time or another. When one faces these questions, it is usually done with great fear and trepidation.

Over the years I have talked with many individuals facing these questions and most of them approached the subject with great anxiety. Why? Because most people think that if I am "called to ministry" that means the Lord is going to send me to some remote part of the world to live in a grass hut and eat worms. Others have made statements like, "I think God is calling me to do something, but I could never speak in front of a group of people." Others fear that the Lord might be calling them, but they feel unworthy to minister to others.

I have great news for you. God **IS** calling **YOU** to ministry. That's right, **YOU**! The Bible clearly teaches us that if you are traveling on *Belief Way* you have been called to minister to others. Let us look at a few examples of what the Lord says about every believer and the call to ministry:

> I, therefore, the prisoner of the Lord, beseech you to walk worthy of the calling with which you were called, with all lowliness and gentleness, with longsuffering, bearing with one another in love. Ephesians 4:1-2

> As each one has received a gift, minister it to one another, as good stewards of the manifold grace of God. 1 Peter 4:10

> Having then gifts differing according to the grace that is given to us, let us use them... Romans 12:6a

Each of these passages of Scripture are found in a context where the author is speaking to all believers, not just those in some sort of special service. We have come to think of those who are in the position of pastor, missionary, music pastor, youth pastor, etc. as ministers and everyone else in the Church as some other class of Christian. However, a careful study of the New Testament gives a different picture altogether. The fact is, Jesus has called all believers to be ministers.

Though we are **all** called to minister, we are not all called to be pastors, seminary professors, or church planters. Though we are **all** called to minister, we are not all called to move to another town, state, or country. In fact, if you study the context of each of the passages mentioned earlier, you will find that we have various offices of ministry to fulfill right where we live.

> For as we have many members in one body, but all members do not have the same function, so we being many are one body in Christ, and individually members of one another. Romans 12:4-5

> And He Himself gave some to be apostles, some prophets, some evangelists, and some pastors and teachers, for the equipping of the saints for the work of ministry, for the edifying of the body of Christ. Ephesians 4:11-12

> For as the body is one and has many members, but all the members of that one body, being many, are one body so also is Christ...For in fact the body is not one member but many. If the foot should say, "Because I am not the hand, I am not of the body" is it therefore not of the body? If the whole body were an eye, where would be the hearing? If the whole were hearing, where would be the smelling? But now God has set the members, each one of them, in the body just as he pleased. 1 Corinthians 12:12, 14-18

If you have trusted Jesus as your Savior, then not only are you traveling *Belief Way*, but you are a part of the Body of Christ. The Body of Christ is seen in the world through the local New

Testament church, and you should be a part of that local Body of Believers. When you join a church, you are not just joining an organization, but an organism. You are joining a local expression of the Body of Christ. As a part of that Body, the Lord has called you to minister in a certain capacity and He has gifted you and will empower you to fulfill the task He has given. **You** have been **called by God** to **minister** to others!

THE CONDUCT OF MINISTRY

Once it is established that we are all called by God to minister to others, several questions remain. What kind of ministry am **I** to be involved in? How **should I** conduct my ministry? How **can I** conduct my ministry? The Lord has answered these and other related questions for us in His Word. His Word is our guide to all areas of ministry.

There are four primary texts of Scripture that deal with the issue of the believer's ministry. They are Romans 12, 1 Corinthians 12-14, Ephesians 4, and 1 Peter 4. We have already considered a few ideas from each of these texts, but we will now turn our attention to a brief examination of each passage.

Romans 12

This chapter deals extensively with the issues of ministry and the believer. There are three main points that this passage makes. First, we must heed the spiritual guidelines. Second, we must use the spiritual gifts. Third, we must maintain a spiritual guard.

We Must Heed the Spiritual Guidelines

In the first 5 verses of this chapter, we are given three specific commands that are to serve as important guidelines in carrying out our daily ministry as Christians. The first command, found in verse 1, is to present our bodies to the Lord. We are to present our bodies 1) As a living sacrifice, 2) Holy, and 3) Acceptable to God. The idea of a living sacrifice is that we are to yield ourselves completely to the Lord. Holy means to be separate or distinct, thus, we are to be distinct from the world we live in. In other words, we are to be **in** but not **of** the world. This is the only way that believers can present themselves to God in an acceptable manner. It is unacceptable to present ourselves to the Lord partially, half-heartedly, or sinfully.

The second commandment given to us as a guideline for ministry is found in verse 2. "And do not be conformed to this world, but be transformed by the renewing of your mind, that you may prove what is that good and acceptable and perfect will of God." We are faced everyday with the pressure to conform our lives to the lifestyles of the world around us. Yet, we are to refuse to conform to the world by allowing the Lord to continually transform us into faithful children of God. This transformation takes place through the renewing of our minds. Our minds are renewed, as we grow closer to the Lord through concentration on His Word and time spent in conversation with Him. By obeying this command, you prove God's good, acceptable, and perfect will for your life.

The third command that serves as a guide to us in Christian ministry is found in verse 3. "Though the grace given to me, to everyone who is among you, not to think of himself more highly than he ought to think, but to think soberly, as God has dealt to each one a measure of faith." We are to realize that God has given specific roles for each of us to fill, and no one member is more important to the Body than any other member. We all have different functions, but we are one Body in Christ, working as a unit to fulfill the will of the Lord (Rom 12:4-5).

We Must Use the Spiritual Gifts

In verses 6-8 of this chapter, we are encouraged to use the spiritual gifts the Lord has given to us. The passage lists several of the gifts; however, the list is not exhaustive, it is a sample list. Prior to listing some of the spiritual gifts it is indicated that we have differing gifts, "according to the grace that is given to us." In other words, not everyone has the same gift, but God gives us the gifts that He chooses according to His grace. Notice also that even before the gifts are listed, we are told to use the gifts God has given us.

The list begins in the later part of verse six. If God has given us the spiritual gift of prophecy, we are to use it for His glory in proportion to our faith. The gift of prophecy in this context has to do with "forth-telling" not "foretelling". Thus, the person with this gift is to be faithful to tell forth the Word of God. The gift of ministry as used in this context refers specifically to the act of service. Some individuals will never be involved in public speaking, but they serve the Lord by serving others. The gift of teaching is the gift of detailed instruction of God's Word. The gift of exhortation is the gift of practical encouragement based on God's Word. The gift of giving is the gift of extra ordinary giving of time and finances to the Lord's work and the Lord's people. The gift of leadership has to do with administration and organization. The gift of mercy is that special God – given ability to listen, sympathize, and even empathize with others.

We Must Maintain a Spiritual Guard

In the final section of this chapter, we find the Apostle Paul encouraging his readers to be on guard for some common pitfalls in using spiritual gifts. He begins in verse 9 with a warning to those with the gift of mercy and continues in backward order to give instructive warnings to those with each of the gifts.

Those with the gift of mercy must let "love be without hypocrisy." Sometimes individuals with this gift show mercy to the extent that they ignore sin in the lives of others. We must love others, even those living in sin, but at the same time we must "abhor what is evil" and "cling to what is good."

Those with the gift of leadership or administration must lead with brotherly love. They must not bring honor upon themselves, but bring honor upon those they lead. They must give preference to those they lead instead of placing their own interests at the forefront.

Those with the gift of giving must exercise their gift with diligence. They must not give just to give, but they must give out of a fervent spirit. The giving must be done as an act of ministry or service to the Lord, rather than just giving to any cause that may arise out of a sense of duty.

The encourager must be careful to always rejoice in the hope of the Lord. He must remember that God is at work in the life of His children and that He will complete the work He started. Thus, there is always reason for hope. He must be patient and persevere as he exhorts others around him.

The teacher, though motivated by and dedicated to the careful study of the Word of God, must not rely on his own ability to study, prepare, and communicate. The teacher must realize the power to convey truth and see lives changed comes from time alone with God. Thus, the one with this gift must be continually faithful in prayer.

The servant, those with the gift of serving one another, must seek to meet the needs of the saints and be given to hospitality. These individuals love to serve others for the sake of the Lord. Many times, their service goes unnoticed, but they must be faithful to minister without partiality.

Many times, those with the gift of prophecy come across very forthright. They spot sin in their own lives as well as the lives of others very quickly and they do not hesitate to make it known. They must be careful to love those who are persecuting them. They must take care to rejoice when it is appropriate. They must speak the truth in love.

1 Corinthians 12-14

The Corinthian church was suffering from division. There were many issues that divided this congregation of believers, one of which was spiritual gifts. There was a group of believers who had chosen one gift and attempted to make it the primary gift. In fact, they held it in such esteem that anyone who did not have this gift was left out. In the three chapters at hand, the Lord led the Apostle Paul to deal with the abuse of spiritual gifts by establishing several important principles.

Chapter 12 teaches three primary principles: 1) There are several different gifts, 2) The Holy Spirit determines who gets what gifts, 3)The church is One Body in Christ with many members who do not all have the same function. Chapter 13 deals with 1 essential principle: without love, spiritual gifts mean nothing. Chapter 14 discusses specific issues of the abuse of the gift of tongues in the Corinthian church. The main principle of this chapter is that the true purpose of spiritual gifts is to edify (build up) other believers.

Chapter 12

The first two spiritual gift principles discussed in this chapter are found in the first paragraph, verses 1-11. The Apostle begins the chapter by reminding his readers that all true believers have the Holy Spirit and there is just one Holy Spirit. The Spirit works through all believers for the profit of all believers. He then states that though there is only one Spirit, there are several different spiritual gifts. In verses 8-10 Paul listed nine different gifts. This list, like the one in Romans 12, is not a complete list but it is a sample list. The principle is that there are several different spiritual gifts, not just one or two.

This paragraph also teaches another important principle about spiritual gifts. A careful look at the listing of gifts will reveal a statement that is repeated several times, "by the same Spirit." The idea is that the Holy Spirit is the one who gives spiritual gifts to the believer and thus He, and He alone, determines who receives what gift. This principle is stated clearly in the final verse of the paragraph, verse 11. **"But one and the same Spirit works all these things, distributing to each one individually as He will."**

The second paragraph draws on the imagery of the body to teach us the third principle of the chapter. Just as the human body has many parts and is one unit, so the Body of Christ, the Church, is One Body with many different parts. All parts do not look alike, and all parts do not have the same function within the body. So, with the Church, not all members have the same spiritual gift or function within the body. If every part of the human body were an eye, we would not be able to function properly. In the same way, if every believer in a particular church had the same gift, the Body of Christ would not be able to function properly. We are one body with many members and several gifts, functions, and offices. Yet we work together for the glory of God by evangelizing the sinner, edifying the saint, and exalting the Savior.

Chapter 13

Many believers are familiar with this chapter, often referred to as *the Love Chapter*. What many are not familiar with is the context in which this chapter is found. In the midst of the Corinthian controversy over spiritual gifts, some members had lost their love for one another. They were treating each other with contempt and were in danger of an all-out church split. Thus, the Apostle reminds them that without love we are nothing.

The chapter can easily be understood when we see the three main points established. In verses 1-3 we learn of the necessity of love. No matter what spiritual gift one has or what action one takes, without love he/she is nothing. In verses 4-8 the characteristics of true (agape) love are given. The Bible's description of true love stands in contrast to the world's ideas of love. Verses 9-13 teach that love is eternal. Even spiritual gifts, as we know them, will cease but love will last for all of eternity.

Chapter 14

This chapter deals with the specific issue they were facing at Corinth, the abuse of the gift of tongues. In verses 1-5 Paul told them that they were using the gift to build up self, instead of building up others, which is God's intended use of all spiritual gifts. In verses 6-19 he gave an example of this abuse. Then in verses 20-25 the Apostle further contrasts the purpose of the gift and the abuse of it in the Corinthian congregation. Finally, Paul gives the needed correction in verses 26-40. The overarching principle of the entire chapter is that spiritual gifts are to edify (build up) others, not ourselves.

Ephesians 4

The first 16 verses of this chapter deal with spiritual gifts and the Body of Christ. In verses 1-3 the readers are told to Live Worthy. Then in verses 4-16 they are told to Live as One. The first section of this passage talks of living according to our individual calling. The second section deals with the different parts of the Body living in harmony while living out their particular calling and function.

Live Worthy

Verse 1 gives us the command to live worthy of the calling God has given to each of us as believers. Verses 2-3 tell us how to be obedient to the command. We can live worthy by using our spiritual gift with lowliness (humility), gentleness, longsuffering (patience), bearing with one another, and working to keep unity within the Body through the "bond of peace." We are not to expect all believers to have the same gift as we have or to emphasize the same things we emphasize. We are to recognize and rejoice in the differences while seeking to maintain Biblical unity.

Live as One

In verses 4-16 there are two primary thoughts conveyed. First, the reader is reminded that we are One Body in verses 4-6. Then in verses 7-16 the readers are told that we are individuals with various God-given roles and functions within the body, which we are to carry out in order for the Body to be edified. In this section a few spiritual gifts are listed, they are: apostles, prophets, evangelists, and pastor/teachers. Each of these have a specific role in "**equipping the saints for the work of ministry, for edifying of the body of Christ.**" Thus, it is the pastor's job to help members understand their gifts and to equip them to carry out the work of the ministry so that the Body will be edified.

1 Peter 4

Around AD 63, under the inspiration of the Holy Spirit, the Apostle Peter wrote the book we know as 1 Peter. He was nearing his time of execution for the cause of Christ, and he wanted to leave some instructions for believers. In this epistle he deals with several important issues that believers face. In chapter 4 verses 7-11, Peter wrote concerning the believer and ministry through spiritual gifts. He began the paragraph by stating that we are living in the last days. He then turns his attention to four commands that are essential for believers. First, he said to be serious and watchful in prayer, second to love one another, third to be hospitable, and fourth to minister to one another.

The command to minister to one another is found in verses 10-11. The Apostle does not go into much detail, but he gives a powerful message. The message can be summed up this way: As a good steward of God's grace, use the gift you have been given to bring glory to the Lord. Peter does not list any of the gifts, but he does give us two main divisions of the gifts. There are speaking gifts like prophet, teacher, evangelist, etc. and there are ministry gifts like servant, administrator, mercy shower, etc. No matter what your gift is, you must understand that it has been given to you by the Lord and you must use it to glorify Him.

Concluding Considerations

Scripture is clear that the Lord has called every believer to active ministry within the Body of Christ. Thus, ministry is a mandate. We have various gifts to carry out this ministry. Our gifts were given by the Holy Spirit to enable us to edify one another and bring glory to God. We are to use our gifts faithfully as a member of the One Body of Christ. When we use our gifts to fulfill the ministry given to us by God, we grow in our walk with Him.

Two questions remain: 1) What is your gift or gifts? And 2) How can you use them in your present setting? There are several spiritual gift studies that have been designed to help you learn what your gift is and how you can apply that gift to God's work in your area. Your first step should be to speak with your pastor, deacon, and/or small group leader about spiritual gifts. They will be able to help you find your place of ministry within the Body.

Discussion Questions

1. Who has been called by God and given a mandate to ministry?
2. What are the main passages of Scripture that teach us about Spiritual Gifts?
3. Where do Spiritual Gifts come from and who determined what gifts(s) I have?
4. What is the purpose of Spiritual Gifts?

CHAPTER 8

Growth Must Be Ongoing

If you have ever taken a long trip with children, there is a question that you are very familiar with. *"Are we there yet?"* On the first long trip I remember taking I am sure I must have asked that question more times than my parents could have counted. Why? Because it was an extensive trip, and I was not used to being in the car for such a long time. Sometimes as believers on the road to Christian maturity, we feel the urge to ask that same question. *"Are we there yet?"*

Traveling the road to maturity as a believer is no quick trip to the corner store; it is a lifelong journey. The journey begins at the moment that you trust Jesus as your Lord and Savior and continues to the day that you meet Him face to face in Heaven. In the beginning of your journey, you have fellow Christians who take responsibility to help you to grow. As time passes, you take on more and more of the responsibility for your own growth. Soon you begin to not only take responsibility for your own growth, but you help others to grow as well. Yet, no matter how long it has been since one began to travel on *Belief Way*, your growth will be an ongoing process throughout all of life.

In this chapter we will consider four aspects concerning this ongoing process of growth. First, we will consider *The Obligation to Grow*. Second, we will examine *The Obstacles to Growth*. Third, we will discuss *The Atmosphere of Growth*. Finally, we will take a look at *The Accomplishment of Growth*.

THE OBLIGATION TO GROW

> You therefore, beloved, since you know this before-hand, beware lest you also fall from your own stead-fastness, being led away with the error of the wicked; but grow in the grace and knowledge of our Lord and Savior Jesus Christ. To Him be the glory both now and forever. Amen (2 Peter 3:17-18).

These words conclude the Apostle Peter's writings. He was near his time of martyrdom and he wrote the letter we know as 2 Peter to encourage His fellow believers to remain faithful during difficult times. He began the epistle by commanding his readers to grow in 1:5-11 and then he spoke of the trustworthiness of God's Word. In chapter two, Peter warned about false teachers. Chapter three is made up of three paragraphs. In verses 1-9 he considers the fact that God is not slack concerning his promises. In verses 10-13 the Apostle discusses "the day of the Lord." Then in verses 14-18 he contrasted those who are untaught and unstable with those who remain steadfast.

The concluding verse, printed above, gives a command to those who would remain steadfast. In this context we learn that if one is to be steadfast, they must not stand still. To be steadfast, we must grow. This growth must be in two areas: 1) the grace of our Lord and 2) the knowledge of our Lord.

Grow in Grace

To grow in the grace of the Lord is to walk in the reality of His grace day-by-day, moment-by-moment. We are to walk with the Lord in the same way we received Him, by grace through faith. May we grow *through* His grace and may we grow *in the expression* of His grace to others.

Grow in Knowledge

Peter also said that we are to grow in the knowledge of the Lord. You can know about the Lord without ever really knowing Him. However, you cannot really know the Lord without knowing about Him. I know about Abraham Lincoln, but I do not know Him. I know my wife, Cindy Ballard, and thus, I also know about her as well. Notice the command of Peter is that we grow in our knowledge of the Lord. The idea is to grow in our knowledge of *Him*, not just *facts about Him*. As we grow in our relationship with Him we will know more about Him, but more than that, we will know Him better than before. As we grow in His grace and in our knowledge of Him we will bring glory to Him "both now and forever."

Remember that verse 18 is a direct command given to each believer, not simply a suggestion. This command is given by our

Lord, through the hand of Peter. Therefore, we are obligated to obey it. We are obligated to grow, and that growth is a continuous process from the day we trust Jesus as our Lord and Savior until the day we meet Him face to face.

THE OBSTACLES OF GROWTH

Just as growing children experience "growing pains" so do growing believers. As one matures in the faith, obstacles will arise to get us off track in our growth process. When obstacles arise, we must know how to deal with them. Sometimes the obstacle will be small, sometimes large, but one thing is always true of obstacles. Obstacles can hinder our growth, or they can be used by God to spur us on to greater growth. Though each obstacle we face may look different than the one before, there are three general categories from which obstacles arise.

The Obstacle of Sin

Sin is an obstacle to growth. If we have unconfessed sin in our lives, our growth process comes to a halt until it is dealt with. King David was called "a man after God's own heart" yet, he went through an entire year of spiritual drought. His growth in the Lord came to a quick halt when he sinned with Bathsheba and had her husband killed. For about a year, he "kept silent" (Psalms 3:23). Then Nathan, the prophet of the Lord, came to the king and confronted him with his sin. David confessed his sin before the Lord. This confession is found in Psalm 51. Once the sin was confessed, David was back on the road to spiritual maturity, though he still faced the consequences and scars of his sin.

When we give in to sin, our growth to Christian maturity comes to a halt as well. As long as we ignore the sin, we stunt our growth. However, when we confess our failures to the Lord, He will forgive us and put us back on the path of spiritual growth. "**If we confess our sins, He is faithful and just to forgive us our sins and to cleanse us from all unrighteousness**" (1 John 1:9).

The Obstacle of Self

The Apostle Paul referred to self as "the old man" (Rom 6:6). This is that sin nature that causes the struggle of right and wrong within the believer. The "old man" wants to put self first and make decisions based on what makes the "old man" feel good. The "new man" (Col 3:10) desires to please our Heavenly Father with simple obedience. When we give in to self, we hinder our growth in the Lord.

Paul reminds us in Romans 6 that we were united with Christ in his death and resurrection. Thus, our "old man" has been crucified with Christ and we now have the "new man" living within us. Jesus has given us the victory over self. We must simply claim and walk in that victory.

The Obstacle of Satan

Peter, in his first epistle, warned his readers concerning the devil. He said, "**Be sober, be vigilant; because your adversary the devil walks about like a roaring lion, seeking whom he may devour**" (1 Peter 5:8). The devil will do anything he can to place obstacles in the path to growth. He does not want believers to experience spiritual growth. He will tempt you, scare you, depress you, etc. to slow your progress. But the good news is that Jesus already won the victory over Satan and that victory can be yours. **"Resist him, steadfast in the faith, knowing that the same sufferings are experienced by your brotherhood in the world"** (1 Peter 5:9). James echoed Peter's admonition, **"Therefore submit to God, Resist the devil and he will flee from you"** (James 4:7). As we submit ourselves to God, we can have victory over the devil and continue on the path of Christian maturity.

The Atmosphere of Growth

Just as good weather makes a long road trip more enjoyable and productive, so a good atmosphere for growth will make your journey on *Belief Way* more enjoyable and productive. We must take care to make sure that we are in an atmosphere conducive to spiritual growth. A careful study of the New Testament reveals that our Lord has provided a place for our growth to be enhanced. That place is the local church. However, not every church has an atmosphere of growth. Acts 2:40-47 describes the early Church and in this description we find the characteristics that are essential for a congregation to provide an atmosphere of growth.

> And with many other words he testified and exhorted them, saying, "Be saved from this perverse generation." Then those who gladly received his word were baptized; and that day about three thousand souls

were added to them. And they continued steadfastly in the apostles' doctrine and fellowship, in the breaking of bread, and in prayers. Then fear came upon every soul, and many wonders and signs were done through the apostles. Now all who believed were together, and had all things in common, and sold their possessions and goods, and divided them among all, as anyone had need. So continuing daily with one accord in the temple, and breaking bread from house to house, they ate their food with gladness and simplicity of heart, praising God and having favor with all the people. And the Lord added to the church daily those who were being saved.

There are three main characteristics revealed in this text, which are essential for a church to provide the right kind of atmosphere for spiritual growth. The first is found in verses 40-41. In these verses we find that the Church *evangelized sinners*. From the context of the chapter, we find that Peter led in sharing the Gospel, but all the early believers were involved in evangelism.

The second essential characteristic is found in verses 42-46. Here we find that the Church *edified the saints*. There was a mutual building up of one another as believers. This edification was accomplished through Biblical teaching, Biblical fellowship, Biblical worship, Biblical prayer, and Biblical care.

The third characteristic is found in the first two words of verse 47. "**Praising God**" together is essential to proper spiritual growth. We must *exalt the Savior*. We can praise God through spoken testimony or through musical testimony. God is to be praised for Who He is, what He has done, what He is doing, and what He is going to do.

When a congregation is characterized by these three essentials: *evangelizing the sinners, edifying the saints,* and *exalting the Savior*; it is providing a wonderful atmosphere for growth. Each individual believer is responsible to make sure that he/she is involved in such a church. The proper atmosphere for growth will make the journey on *Belief Way* more enjoyable and productive.

THE ACCOMPLISHMENT OF GROWTH

We began this chapter by considering our obligation to grow. We are commanded to **"grow in the grace and knowledge of our Lord and Savior Jesus Christ."** (2 Peter 3:18). However, let me assure you that if you have truly come to the place of trusting Jesus as your Savior, you will grow in your faith and one day you will reach Christian maturity. In the book of Philippians, the Apostle Paul gave us a promise from the Lord concerning the completion of our growth process. He wrote, **"being confident of this very thing, that He who has begun a good work in you will complete it until the day of Jesus Christ"** (Phil 1:6).

The fact is, the Lord has promised that if He begins a good work in someone, He will complete it. At the moment of salvation Jesus began a good work in your life and He always finishes what He starts. At times you may resist or even rebel, but His work will come to a completion. He will convict you, chasten you, and discipline you until you grow in your walk with Him.

If you have entered *Belief Way*, He will never leave you and He will make certain that you reach the destination of Christian maturity. If you get stalled out on the side of the road, He will pick you up and get you going again. If you drive the wrong way in a one-way lane for a period of time, He will turn you around and get you heading in right direction once again. Whatever it takes, He will make sure that you grow. Realizing His marvelous grace, let us be His partners in our growth process, instead of driving against the flow of traffic on *Belief Way*.

Discussion Questions

1. In what two areas are we commanded to grow?
2. What does it mean to grow in the grace of our Lord?
3. What does it mean to grow in the knowledge of our Lord?
4. Name three obstacles to growth.
5. What institution did the Lord ordain to provide an atmosphere of growth?
6. What are three characteristics essential to this atmosphere?
7. How can we be sure that every true believer will reach Christian Maturity?

REFERENCE NOTES

1   https://news.gallup.com/poll/393737/belief-god-dips-new-
    low.aspx#:~:text=WASHINGTON%2C%20D.C.%20
    %2D%2D%20The%20vast,the%20lowest%20in%20Gal-
    lup's%20trend. Accessed April 20, 2024.
2   Dr. D. James Kennedy popularized these three categories in
    his Evangelism Explosion witness training.
3   Several teachers and authors have used different versions
    of the bridge illustration including Bill Bright in his
    teaching and print materials.
4   Dr. Daniel Akin, Systematic Theology Class Notes, South-
    eastern Baptist Theological Seminary, Wake Forest, NC,
    1992.
5   Thayer, *Greek-English Lexicon of the New Testament*, Baker
    Book House, Grand Rapids, MI. p. 352.

OTHER TITLES BY MARK BALLARD

When did you last hear a sermon about the Rapture or the End Times? Pastor, when did you last preach about the Rapture or the End Times? If it has been months or even years, does it really matter? What is the Rapture? How is it defined? When will the Rapture happen? If the Rapture happens today, how can you be sure you will not be left behind? For answers to these and many more important questions, read the inspiring, encouraging, and comforting book, *Does the Rapture Still Matter?*

Words matter. How we use them and define them determines how we understand the world and how others understand us. In *Words Matter: What Is the Gospel?* Drs. Mark H. Ballard and Timothy K. Christian explore how our personal definition of the word "Gospel" fundamentally affects our view of the world, our lives, and our standing with God.

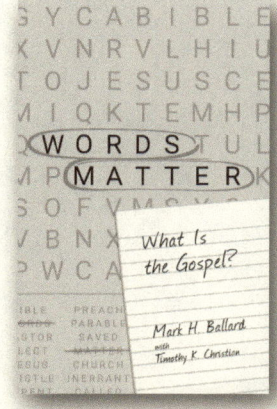

It has been noted that two men did more for Biblical Christianity in the 19th century than any other: Charles Haddon Spurgeon and Dwight Lyman Moody. The influence of D. L. Moody continues today. While much has been written about this great man of God, very little has been published about his preaching. This volume exposes a little-known fact: though Moody began as a topical speaker, he became a text-driven preacher in his later years.

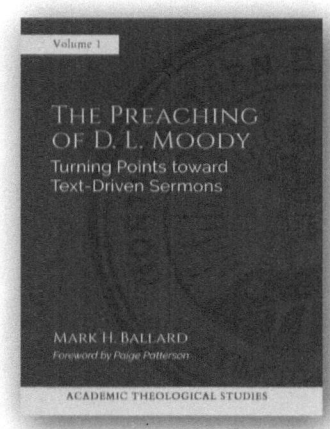

Normal's Journey is a fascinating and compelling description of one man's search for satisfaction and fulfilment. Through his search, he discovers that the dissatisfaction that overwhelmed his life is rooted in his lack of intimacy with his Lord Jesus Christ. His journey-Normal's Journey-is our own story, of seeking the full life found only in Christ.

Priorities: Reaching the Life God Intended grew out of Dr. Mark Ballard's long-term study and experience. For Ballard, priorities changed an expected high school dropout into class valedictorian. Priorities helped him earn a college degree, two graduate degrees, and become a college founder and president. Along the way, priorities helped him plant and pastor multiple churches. What can priorities do for you?